HEALING NATURE

BY THE SAME AUTHOR

Poetry

Collected Poems 1960–1984

Plays

Maquettes (a trilogy of one-act plays)
Lying Figures (Part One of REQUIEM, a trilogy)
Killing Time (Part Two of REQUIEM)
Meeting Ends (Part Three of REQUIEM)
A Conception of Love
Light Shadows
Moving Reflections
Living Creation
Healing Nature

Editor

Eleven Poems by Edmund Blunden
Garland
Studies in the Arts

HEALING NATURE

The Athens of Pericles

a play by Francis Warner

οὔτοι συνέχθειν ἀλλὰ συμφιλεῖν ἔφυν
Sophocles, *Antigone*

OXFORD THEATRE TEXTS 9

COLIN SMYTHE, GERRARDS CROSS, 1988

British Library Cataloguing in Publication Data

Warner, Francis, *1937–*
Healing Nature : the Athens of Pericles :
a play. — (Oxford theatre texts; 9)
I. Title II. Series
822′.914
ISBN 0–86140–270–7

First published in 1988 by Colin Smythe Ltd.,
Gerrards Cross, Buckinghamshire

Distributed in North America by
Dufour Editions, P.O. Box 449, Chester Springs, PA 19425

Portrait of Pericles by Lucy Warner
Cover design and production photograph by
Billet Potter of Oxford

Produced in Great Britain

FOR PENELOPE

HEALING NATURE was commissioned by the Oxford University Dramatic Society (OUDS) for performance in the Sheldonian Theatre, Oxford on Friday, November 20th, 1987. The play and the production were sponsored by Adamantios Lemos. The director was Mark Payton.

The cast was as follows:

Megakles	*Matthew Blakstad*
Euangelos	*Noel Waddington*
Kallias	*Andrew Warmington*
Pericles	*Rob Smith*
Kleinias	*Richard Lloyd Parry*
Sophocles	*Mark Payton*
Pindar	*Simon Beaufoy*
Kimon	*Richard Smith*
Xanthippos	*Anthony Eyers*
Ephialtes	*Tim Tzouliadis*
Anaxagoras	*Noel Waddington*
Euripides	*Matthew Blakstad*
Thukydides	*Richard Smith*
Diopeithes	*Tim Tzouliadis*
Lampon	*Andrew Warmington*
Xanthippos Jnr.	*Simon Beaufoy*
Perichore	*Bethany Bell*
Aspasia	*Bridget Foreman*
Eterapoula	*Francesca Lepper*
Elpinike	*Rebecca Ockenden*

Others parts played by members of the Company, which included Nancy Elmore, Michael Harmon, Dana Reynolds, Denis Thomopoulos.

Stage Manager Claudine Lim. Costumes Shirley Reece. Props Gill Cain. Lighting David Colmer. Electricians Julian Gale, Crispin Marriott. Poster and programme designed by Lucy Warner. Producer Toby Davies.

Characters

First Prologue
Second Prologue

Megakles	*Uncle of Pericles*
Euangelos	*Steward of Pericles, a slave*
Kallias	*Ambassador, Torchbearer of the Eleusinian Mysteries*
Pericles	
Kleinias	*Soldier, son-in-law of Megakles*
Sophocles	*General and Dramatist*
Pindar	*Poet*
Herald	
Kimon	*General, Conservative Leader*
Xanthippos	*Father of Pericles*
Ephialtes	*Leader of the Opposition*
Anaxagoras	*Philosopher, tutor of Pericles*
Euripides	*Dramatist*
Thukydides	*Kimon's brother-in-law*
Diopeithes	*a studier of oracles*
Lampon	*a Seer*
Xanthippos Jnr.	*Son of Pericles*
Perichore	*(four syllables) a Courtesan*
Aspasia	*a Courtesan, consort of Pericles*
Eterapoula	*a Courtesan*
Elpinike	*(four syllables) Kimon's sister, wife of Kallias*

Athenian Citizens

The Play is set in the middle years of the fifth century B.C.

Act One: Delphi. Acts Two, Three and Four: Athens.

PROLOGUES

FIRST *spoken by actor playing* PERICLES: SECOND *by actor playing* SOPHOCLES.

FIRST To earn the future we must learn from past
Mistakes, and triumphs, or be frivolous.
Society needs memory to last:
Today makes history, but it made us.

SECOND We know more than they did.

FIRST Yes, that is true;
And they are what we know.

SECOND Each life consists
Of roots. However much we misconstrue,
The music of the mysteries persists.

FIRST 'What sort of people' once Odysseus asked
'Are these? Barbarians? Arrogant? Unfair?
Or friends to strangers, fearing God?'

SECOND Unmasked,
Relying on your goodwill, we are here,
And offer you, hoping that it may please,

FIRST Our play of Athens and her Pericles.

Act One

SCENE ONE

MEGAKLES

The lamps that hang down from the frosty height,
Those wheeling stars that keep eternal time,
Pale eastward over Athens as the dawn,
Drowsy at Delphi on this mountainside,
Slowly, with soft elation, strokes the skies
And forests from the darkness. Quiet snow
On far Olympus shapes one crystal less
While last remaining scudding storm-clouds pass,
Birds wheel and turn in the sky like bees or gnats,
And trees, with their enormous dignity
At dusk and dawn, the fir and juniper,
White pine and beech, stand black in silhouette
Against full rising splendour of new day.
This last of eight days of the Pythian Games
In honour of Apollo shall be mine.
My horses weave their heads and scrape the ground
(All four are god-like), and my chariot
With which we Alkmaeonidae have won
Seven victories, and one, greatest of all:
The Four-Horse Prize at god's Olympic Games,
Is ready. Come, Euangelos my boy;
You've served me well, and kept all my accounts
This week. Now I will lift you in the world
And recommend you to my rising nephew—
My loved, late sister Agariste's son—
Pericles. Have we any more to do?

EUANGELOS

Great Megakles, there is one thing I'd ask . . .

MEGAKLES

Speak on, young man.

EUANGELOS Why have you been exiled,
Ostracized for ten years from your own Athens?

MEGAKLES Envy requiting fine deeds; these things happen.
My uncle Kleisthenes the Law-Giver,
In order to prevent new tyrannies,
Gave the Assembly of the People power
To send to honourable exile those
Whose names they scratched on bits of pottery.
Now it has been misused. What threat was I?

EUANGELOS Themistocles was highest in the state
For a brief while; on his decline, struck you.

MEGAKLES Themistocles, that traitor to our class
Incited the sea-rabble with my name—
Spelled it for them; and triumphed. But soon he
Was ostracized, for all his lizard tongue,
Indicted by our Alkmaeonidae;
And now he vaults to Greece's enemy
The Great King of the Persians—Artaxerxes,
Vented by the wise Areopagus.

EUANGELOS He built our navy; won us Salamis;
Walled the Piraeus, gave the sailors votes.

MEGAKLES The trireme rowers? That was Aristeides.
High Zeus! He too—'The Just'—was ostracized.
Oh Athens! All your greatest sons you spurn.

EUANGELOS At least they don't dissolve your property.

Trumpet.

MEGAKLES The horses! There is generous Kallias,
The richest man in Athens, honoured here
At Delphi, not because he's torchbearer
Of sister mysteries at Eleusis,
Nor that he's been to Susa, Artaxerxes'
Capital rich with hoarded treasure, as
Ambassador for Athens. He's won three
Olympic victories with his chariot teams!

EUANGELOS He fought at Marathon.

MEGAKLES It made him rich.

EUANGELOS You mean his nickname 'Buried Booty'? Well,
Aeschylus fought . . .

MEGAKLES *This* man's an aristocrat!

KALLIAS May bright Apollo gild your race today,
Alkmaeonid! The goat-bells and the spring
Castalian splashing down the mountainside
Reflect and echo: 'Megakles has won!'
And all the syllables on every tree,
In every hidden heart, thank your great clan
For building this proud temple.

MEGAKLES Kallias,
Thank Xanthippos; there's his son, Pericles!
This young man is to run all the estates
Of Pericles, to leave him free for Athens.
Show him the texture of his master's mind.

Trumpet.

My horses call!

KALLIAS May the Far-Darting One
Sustain you!

Exit MEGAKLES.

He's the third one of that name,
'Megakles'.

EUANGELOS Was the old temple burnt?

KALLIAS It was.
The Alkmaeonidae honoured Apollo
(And Dionysus in the winter months)
In the rebuilding programme, which required
Only free stone. They gave this great façade
Of Parian marble.

EUANGELOS Paros!

KALLIAS Yes.

EUANGELOS My home!

Enter PERICLES.

Paros, that perfect island out to sea
In the Aegean of the Cyclades,
Sand-rich and marble-mountained, feels a sky
Spangled with stars, where cloudless soft winds shelter
From all the storms of Athens, and protect
Antiparos, her small lace-necked daughter
Of gold-thread coves, and caverns old as time,
Where vaulted stalactites defend the darkness
Hiding sad echo of Neobule
So loved of salt-teared-cheeked Archilochos.
His poems made her father hang himself;
Before Archilochos himself fought Naxos,
And died on Paros' tideless edge of sand.

KALLIAS Scorpion-tongued Archilochos, more like.
Now, courteous Pericles; what do you think
Of your new steward here?

PERICLES Imagination
Is a rare gift. Ability to think
Things other than they are, and to transform them,
Combined with love of his own native home,
In talismanic words of adolescence,
Endears me to him.

KALLIAS A slave! I'm amazed.

PERICLES Amazement prompts reflection, and defines
Our future action.

Trumpet.

Kallias—our race!

KALLIAS Make sure that he meets Pindar! I must go
To welcome Kimon, here from victory
At Eurymedon. Though he's my brother-in-law—
And you may smile affection perfumes judgement—
Yet even so I say Kimon's the greatest
General that Athens ever had.
On his way there he stopped Naxos seceding:
Surrender-starved the island. There's example
To allies who swear 'Till sunk iron float
We'll help Athens with tribute'—then refuse!

PERICLES My respects to your wife, Elpinike.

Exit KALLIAS.

SCENE TWO

PERICLES Briefly, I'll tell you what you've got to do.
At a fixed date, once every year, sell all
The produce on my lands; sell in advance,
So that the buyers are responsible
For each fresh crop that year—the growing corn,
The vines and olives. Then buy, every day,
All that we need, as poorer people do,
In the plain market.

EUANGELOS That way you control
All that is spent?

PERICLES Exactly; and no time
Is taken up with country managing.
From now on Athens is my wife, since mine
Loyally has returned to her first husband:
Kallias' son, Hipponikos.

EUANGELOS But wasn't
She your cousin? Just an only daughter?

PERICLES Yes. When her father died—you know the law—
And she inherited his great estates,
She had to leave Hipponikos, and come—

Marry her nearest relative—to me.
Now our two sons are grown, as we agreed
She has gone where she loved. I honour her.

SCENE THREE

Shouts of 'Megakles!' Enter KLEINIAS.

KLEINIAS Pericles, look!

PERICLES Debonair Kleinias
Back from the wars! (*To* EUANGELOS) His wife is Megakles' daughter.

KLEINIAS Pythian Apollo's gleaming on his wheels,
And paces him across the vault of heaven.
There are ten chariots: Thessalian;
Aetolian with chestnut colts; milk-white
Mares from Aenia; all yoked, four by four.
They're reined in at the starting line. (*Trumpet*) They're off!

Enter SOPHOCLES.

Sophocles, look!

SOPHOCLES Shod thunder of the sea!
The Krisaean field and all the hippodrome
Break the dawn air with battle harmony
Of straining chariots and wheel-spun dust
Hoof-trampled. Every shaft sweats white with foam.
Helios and Clymene! They're running close.
Each muscle goads with lashed pain to pull clear
The hard-mouthed nostrils and the foaming bit
And drive the whirling press of snorting wheels
And snarling teeth behind. Axles flirt, narrow,
Too kissed for safety. Horses' eyes stretch wide:
Their red blood starts. Boiotian, crouching, feels
Mares' breath corrupt his back—it's flecked with white.
He leans. The rattling deafens up the hills.

The Spartan shaves by Megakles, and leads.
No! Megakles and he close, side by side.
Now one, now the other. Megakles holds back!
Why? Why?

KLEINIAS Because the Spartan has cut in!

SOPHOCLES Oh no!

KLEINIAS And smashed to proud wreck the huge
African
Who climbs the air, caught by the stumbling reins.
Off spin his wheels! The axle javelin-spears
A horse behind. Wreck after wreck shocks in
Sprawling the field.

SOPHOCLES The African is flung
And dragged, like Hector. His head spills its brains.
The pitying crowd cry out to see him die!

KLEINIAS But Megakles is shouting in the ears
Of his Olympic team; his inside trace-horse
Reins in, lets the outer have full play
And clears the post by half an olive as
Eight horses round the lap together! Now
He drives ahead, moves mid-course. Yes—he's
laughing!
Wild mastery!

SOPHOCLES They carry the African
Straight to a pyre to burn him.

KLEINIAS Hear the shout—
He's won!

SCENE FOUR

Enter MEGAKLES *in a chariot drawn by four horses, to cheering. Enter* PINDAR *with* KALLIAS.

MEGAKLES Where is he? Pindar!

PINDAR Here I am.
You win sacred Apollo's laurel wreath.

MEGAKLES Yes, and the right to build my portrait statue
Here in Apollo's Delphic sanctuary,
Templed perpetually where all eyes
Bow, as the wide world visits. Where's my poem?

HERALD The Pythian Priestess and her priests decree
That Kimon, son of great Miltiades,
Marathon's victor; of the house of Ajax,
The Philaïdae; Kimon, who brought back
The bones of Theseus in his trireme from
Pirate-purged Skyros; noble Kimon who
Comes home in victory, loved of all Greece
Having, in the East, at Eurymedon's mouth
Annihilated the whole Persian fleet;
In gratitude we ask you—give the crown
To victor Alkmaeonid Megakles.

Enter KIMON.

KIMON Some say that too much honour paid to men,
Soldiers or athletes, takes from those who fall
In battle, fighting for our safety. Some
Say victory breeds envy, jealousy.
Better envied than pitied! Some protest
No intellectual is praised like this:
Yet who inspires the intellectuals,
Protects them, makes pure excellence the aim?
They doze in autumn's superfluity.
The only danger in outstanding gifts
Is hubris. Then Immortal envy strikes.
But here, as men, beneath the eye of Zeus
We crown our victor. (*Crowns* MEGAKLES) Now,
in highest praise,

Exhilaration, fulfilled mastery,
The instinct gifts of nature, groomed by will,
Caught in a joy that transforms life, transcends
As fire refines dull buried rock to gold,
Or as foul seas blow calm and show the shore,
Or a dreamed goddess wakes your bed, still there;
Or as Demeter (*Bows to* KALLIAS) floods corn
    through the earth
Each spring, or holy Pythoness speaks truths
She could not know, humbling the proud with awe,
We feel the everlasting touch of gods,
And praise Apollo, god of harmony.
Come, Pindar. Use your highest reach of art
In song that gives him immortality.

SCENE FIVE

PINDAR *Solo. Or:*
In verse one, CHORUS *progress down one side.*
In verse two, CHORUS *progress up the other side.*
In verse three, centre stage, they address the victor.

PINDAR'*s Ode*

Athens, proud home, city of Alkmaeonidae,
Best foundation-stone of my chariot-song,
Where in Hellas can greater glory cry
Up to high gods, righters of human wrong?

Athens' citizens built this Parian marble
Porch: and Megakles, you, like your father
Winning hard-fought honour can pass over trouble,
Proud in success. Fortunate pleasure rather

Endows this last day, conquering victor of Python.
Man's delight flowers and falls to the ground soon;
But when Zeus sheds brightness and lifts from
    oblivion,
Life is sweet, the spirit's on honeymoon.

SCENE SIX

EUANGELOS
Pericles, why did your family
Build this façade?

SOPHOCLES
To honour and respect
The gods, with harmony, proportion, grace.

PERICLES
Also to display the great ropes of flax
And papyrus (the Persian army's bridge)
My father leading the Athenian fleet
Brought back from Hellespont—the chains by which
Xerxes had dreamed he'd fetter Europe, when
Asia with his barbarian hordes swept down
Through Macedonia and Thessaly
To be destroyed by us at Salamis.

EUANGELOS
Didn't the Spartan army leaders raise
An eyebrow? Athens had the fleet, but this
At Delphi? And in Athens' name alone?

PERICLES
(*Laughing*) Sophocles led the song of thanksgiving,
Dancing, with lyre in hand.

SOPHOCLES
My greatest moment.
I was sixteen. Nothing will ever match it.

SCENE SEVEN

Enter PINDAR.

PERICLES
Not even your prize at the Dionysia?
Ah, Pindar! Never have you praised so well
As now in song for Megakles.

PINDAR
Good friend!
But Sophocles, what is the truth? Your prize
Has bittered Aeschylus, they say.

SOPHOCLES
Not true!
That gracious man of Marathon far, far
Surpasses me. The archon, Apsephion,
Could see the crowd was splitting into groups;
And such a crowd, when feelings run so high

In such a public contest, can grow ugly.
Instead of choosing judges normally,
By lots, he saw great Kimon, and the Generals
Enter the theatre, and turned to them.
The crowd hushed, knowing what gloved force lay there
And turned near-riot to divinity.
To Dionysus Kimon made oblation,
As all must do who judge, and took the oath.
For three days they sat in the spring-time sun
And on the last, he gave the prize

PINDAR To you!
Your play *Triptolemos* all say was best.

SOPHOCLES Aeschylus, prophet-poet of Eleusis,
Is still beyond our reach, and must be so.
Kimon sets sail for northern, strong-walled Thasos;
That island, near to gold mines on the shore,
Whose silver ore and timber for our ships
She has supplied throughout the Delian League.
Thasos reneges. She has not learned from Naxos!
Athens and allies send ten thousand men
Out from Piraeus, where the hungry crowds
Hammer and push, to build a colony
At Nine Ways on the river Strymon, where
The eye looks out to Thasos. Officers
Have all leave cancelled: you and I must go . . .

PERICLES To Athens, summoned to control the crowds
And power the triremes with keen, hand-picked strength—
Two hundred each, beside the Trierarch
With his four archers, and ten hoplites armed,
Rations, and water. Men sleep at their oars
Crammed close like bees in honeycomb, or swim
For exercise, and to escape the heat.

SOPHOCLES First to Colonos to see my estate,
Then on. We'll meet in Athens! Radiant poet,
Pindar, leave Thebes and sandal-kick with us.

PINDAR Thebes and Aegina need me. Athens can
Protect herself.

PERICLES — She's strong.

PINDAR — At least she's not
Building an Empire, as the Persians are
For tyranny. Hold to your commonwealth.

Exeunt, except Pindar.

SCENE EIGHT

PINDAR — (*Solus*) Oh you, Apollo, with far-shooting darts,
Lord of this glorious shrine that welcomes all
Who climb the winding path Oedipus took
And reach this valley on Parnassus, grant
Our Pericles that best of all delights:
That he may keep to the plain path of life,
And when he dies, leave to his sons a name
Of which no man speaks evil. On the shore
Of Acheron may he turn round and hear
My echoing tongue; for mortal sins are judged
Inexorably by those under earth.
May he who tells the truth, and honours God,
Endure unweeping days.

Exit.

SCENE NINE

XANTHIPPOS — Well, my son. Are you pleased my brother-in-law
Megakles yet again has triumphed?

PERICLES — Yes.
The Alkmaeonidae seem loved at Delphi.

XANTHIPPOS — Funny place, this, my son. The prostitute
Rhodopis donates iron roasting-spits—
There, in a heap behind the altar which
The islanders from Chios dedicate.

PERICLES Pindar loves it, father.

XANTHIPPOS So he should!
He's well paid by the winners of the games.
He wrote a dirge for your grandfather's funeral.
Your mother used to sing it.

PERICLES 'Hippokrates
Like rooted oak held his integrity,
And neither axes nor a Siren could
Frighten, deflect or seduce him from truth.'

XANTHIPPOS Her father was a whole man; give him due,
As Pindar does. We use her family name,
But don't forget my ancestors, my boy,
With all this praise of hers. We Buzygae
Carved deep respect in Athens down the years.

PERICLES Kimon spoke well: except those words against
The intellectuals . . .

XANTHIPPOS He's a good lad.
I may have had to force Miltiades
His father into trial and exile
With fine, but his sound son has never grieved
Or held against me what had to be done.
Why, Kimon served under me at Mycale;
While generous Kallias paid off the fine
And married Kimon's sister, who'd no dower:
Wayward Elpinike.

PERICLES Will that match last?

XANTHIPPOS Come, boy; you think too much. Your friends: that Damon,
Your music teacher—far too radical
For me; like garrulous Heroditus,
And your mad tutor, Anaxagoras—
Good God! Why, he's an atheist!

PERICLES Xanthippos,
Father; please!

XANTHIPPOS They're a bad influence.
You've made your name by paying for that play
By Aeschylus which won the prize.

PERICLES *The Persians*.

XANTHIPPOS Now you should speak in the Assembly, leave
The sodden minds of intellectuals . . .

PERICLES Time, father, is a necessary season
That allows nature to mature and bring
To self-awareness one's identity.

XANTHIPPOS . . . And make your name, boy, as you're starting to,
In military service.

PERICLES My belief
Is that a true Athenian will do both.
Sophocles has become a General;
And Socrates is a good fighting man.

XANTHIPPOS A sophist; nothing more. Born arguer
On any side that comes into his head.
Your mother was intelligent, aware
Politically. She gave wise advice.
She would have had no time for that young man.
Now listen. When I'd locked the Hellespont,
And found those cables that were displayed here,
The Persian Governor of Sestos offered
Two hundred talents to me if I'd spare
His son's life and his own. I took him up
To overlook where Xerxes' bridge had been,
And nailed him to a plank to watch his son
Stoned by a mob to death. I took no bribe.

PERICLES Frailty is as great a leveller
As justice.

XANTHIPPOS Eh? What do you mean?

PERICLES I've learned
Something about myself.

XANTHIPPOS Good! About time.

PERICLES We men of Athens are trained to face death
And not to flinch: merely redeem our name
By fighting to the end. Each one of us
Once in a lifetime at the least will hold
Another human trembling in our power
To kill or spare at our whim. Each of us
Once in a lifetime at the least will be
Completely in the power of someone else
To be killed or be spared. Father, the two
May not be unconnected.

XANTHIPPOS Pericles!
Your elder brother would not think like that;
Nor your young sister, chosen as she is to carry
The sacred basket on Athene's birthday.
There's your mad tutor's bias.

PERICLES Xanthippos:
That is irrelevant.

XANTHIPPOS You need, my boy,
Good barrack-drill with Spartans. Yes! One friend
Of yours I like—he's far too good for you—
King Archidamos down in Sparta, whom
I first met when I went on embassy
For Athens.

PERICLES Yes: that wise and loving man
Is out of place there. He's too good for them.
Themistocles . . .

XANTHIPPOS Themistocles! How dare you
Praise the bear Aristeides and I hunted?

PERICLES I didn't praise, although I admire him—
But Aristeides was your enemy!

XANTHIPPOS True, for a while; but after Salamis
That fox by deme and fox by nature took
Command of all the army, I the fleet

PERICLES Created by Themistocles . . .

XANTHIPPOS What's worse,
You give support to that rat Ephialtes,
That carper after Kimon, who would strike
Our house of lords, the Areopagus,
And strip it of its powers!

PERICLES His name is good.

XANTHIPPOS Same as the traitor at Thermopylae:
Must be a close relation . . .

PERICLES Father; no more.
When I was young you never were at home,
And now I try to listen with respect.
You've grasshoppered the seas with our triremes,
But lost the purpose for which they are sent,
And Homer's wisdom, learned through suffering.
Society does not stand still. I know
That politics is not a life for those
Who value their contentment; yet, I'll try.
When one's tormentor's loved, then self-defence,
Revenge, is self-defeat, and to be hurt
Is to be selfish in its charity.

XANTHIPPOS If ever you reach power, I see the death
Of all in ancient Athens I have loved.
Your mother dreamed she gave a lion birth:
What would she think now if she trod the earth?
Here is my parting curse: may your sons be
The disappointment you have been to me.

END OF ACT ONE

Act Two

SCENE ONE

PERICHORE (*Sola*) The birdsong, the cicadas and the wind
Make me so happy! I could leave this Athens,
And flee as a bird to the mountains, where I'd pick
Lemons, to make my hair grow, whitethorn buds
For diarrhoea, and rosemary for headache—
Oh, what a night! I've singed my body hairs
And feel like a globe thistle. Say Kimon came,
Just on an urge; passing by in the street
Fresh from a battle with his trireme, starved
Of women for a month: 'Yes? Sir! Come in.'
(*Bass voice*) 'Thank you, young beauty.' 'Do you think me so?
You'll make my white complexion blush.' (It's fake.
I use a white lead powder and some rouge.)
'Your arctic saxifrageous cheeks are tinged
With cherry,' (Best for burns) 'and mulberry'
(Mouth ulcers) 'are your round, unbitten nails.'
'Oh, do you like them?' 'Not just them, but you.
The crocus rises and the tulip waves.'
'You make me blush. The snowdrop hangs her head.'
'The King's spear, yellow asphodel commands!'
'What can a lonely periwinkle do
But acquiesce?' 'The elder-flowered orchid
Both short and stout with three lobed lips and spur
Bluntly controls the meadow.' 'But pubescent
Digitalis loves the forest slopes!'
'The heavy-smelling hyacinth climbs fissures
And finds the flat-topped evergreen candytuft.'
'You'll be polite?' 'You must not trust me.' 'Oh!

My bell-flower rings. No, no!' 'Here's shepherd's
    purse:
Speedwell!' Ah! Ah! Ah!

ASPASIA What are you doing?
This is a brothel, not a theatre.
Now, Perichore: will you entertain?

PERICHORE I hate the word, a 'brothel'! That's not us.
We are companions to the politicians.
How do you like my eyelids?

ASPASIA Let me see;
Your azure fringes daylight two tired eyes,
And lost hours slab their weight to pull them down.
Come—take a little rest. I will stay here
Until you wake refreshed. Great men are here.

Exit PERICHORE. *Enter* ETERAPOULA *with* PERICLES *and* EPHIALTES.

ETERAPOULA Aspasia, our women's quarters are
Honoured by Pericles and Ephialtes.

ASPASIA Thanks, Eterapoula—stay with us. Great sirs;
Every ship, every household, needs someone
In charge—and here, where leisure disrobes beauty,
I am she. Here, when man's idea of self
Fails to tally with the outside world,
We lift self-observation from a wound
Into a state of mind that heals, and gives
Transforming confidence. You self-define
Yourselves, you men, by context. When that fails,
We change it for you, and make bud and flower,
Like sculpting water into solid forms,
The private dreams that drive the public man.
Pericles. You are silent.

PERICLES There is a link
Between silence and wonder.

ASPASIA Eterapoula;

You take our incorruptible Ephialtes
There (*To one side of the stage*), into comfort. Pericles,
I'm touched.
Wonder has some potential for desire.

(ASPASIA *and* PERICLES *take the other side of the stage*)

PERICLES You know who I am. Tell me, Aspasia,
How you came by your ways of thought.

ASPASIA Some boats
Come in that are not steered. I sailed one night
From Miletus across a sea of wrecks.
The Persians had dug saps under our walls,
And battering rams and traitors did the rest.
My wounded father went in chains to Susa,
While Hippodamos darkened me away.

PERICLES Eccentric Hippodamos who's rebuilding
Piraeus with his geometric mind.
His plan? A city limited in size
To just ten thousand. All land split in three:
Public, private, divine. Three laws, to cover
Injury, insult, death. Three possible verdicts:
Acquit, condemn, abstain. And, as you've guessed,
Three types of citizen: to work, fight, farm.
Three ways of making love . . .?

ETERAPOULA Yes. The state leaders are corrupted by
Exaggeration of frivolities.

EPHIALTES The ripest moment holds its first decay.
Year after year, when archons give account
Of their high office, and the generals, too,
I will not blunt the hook that parts their lips
Or let pass over in strategic silence
Those grossest faults the people ought to know,
But hack straight questions until they are felled.

PERICLES Kimon proposes
Money or empty ships from any ally
That does not want to sweat Aegean wars.

ETERAPOULA Well, Solon laid the law down. If your wife's
An heiress, you must love three times a month.
It takes away mislikings and displeasures,
And, if they eat a quince, should breed an heir.

EPHIALTES That's why the Areopagus must go.
What's it consist of? Why, all the ex-archons
Who have cleared or avoided scrutiny.
And there they sit for life, with fattened powers
Just like the Spartans, clean against all we
Have fought for in our new democracy.

ASPASIA Laconic Kimon loves Sparta so much
He's called his son Lakedaimonios.

ETERAPOULA Men choose their girls and politicians by
Their smile and good looks. Ugly Socrates,
Endlessly jabbering in the market-place,
Would never win a democratic vote.

EPHIALTES The crowd can still be patronizingly
Stifled; or bought; or whipped by demagogues
Into a passion; yet, in the long run,
The people know best what's best for the people.

ASPASIA But will our city breed so many fighters?
And what will Delos do with all that wealth?

PERICLES Athens will spend it on the ships and sailors.
Why! Any allied man can join, with pay.

EPHIALTES I controlled thirty ships; Pericles fifty:
But though we looked for action, they were crushed.
When we were under tyrants, our men fought
No better than the next Greek. Now each man
Freely votes his own city's destiny,
Why, even Persia's might is not our match!

ASPASIA The power of love is to transform its object,
And in my case that's sorely what I need.
We can be soaked, or freshened, by the sea
Which wrecks, divides, sustains, and brings new
hope

To alter all direction, till through our folly
Offended nature rises to destroy.

PERICLES Whenever rainclouds billow in the sky,
Or sea-fog rolls along the restless shore
The tossing, strange, incalculable sea,
I'll think of you who are so like my mother,
And have her love of music, and her eyes.
Hope lies in glances at futurity,
And clouds reshape and blend and pile and melt
Till one drop can reflect an entire ocean
Before it forms a part of it. So you.

ETERAPOULA Well, Ephialtes; your thought's nipped with frost,
And a crowd's sympathies can ebb and change.
Kimon will soon be home in triumph. Then
Take care no friends hedgehog your stratagem.

Exit EPHIALTES *and* PERICLES. *Enter* PERICHORE.

PERICHORE Voicing the broken phrases of desire?

ASPASIA Perichore, you're drunk!

PERICHORE (*To* ETERAPOULA) Her tickle leaves
A wound. (*To* ASPASIA) One song? Yes, just one?
Etera, yes?
(*Sings*) One day we'll rule the world, but now we are
Nothing!

ETERAPOULA Nothing!

PERICHORE Nothing!

ETERAPOULA Nothing!

PERICHORE Nothing!

Exeunt.

SCENE TWO

ANAXAGORAS The Greeks are wrong to speak of birth and ending,
Being and perishing, for nothing dies;
Rather, all is compounded or dissolves
From things that are. The atoms rearrange.

PERICLES Why do you say this, Anaxagoras?
Why do you tell me what we've many times
Discussed?

ANAXAGORAS Because, my gentle Pericles,
Now you may need that comfort. Xanthippos,
Your confident father's dead.

PERICLES Xanthippos; father—

ANAXAGORAS The wounds he felt at Sestos took their toll.
He is transformed by that great, infinite
And self-ruled Mind that controls everything
But is itself remote: that cause of motion
Change, disintegration, and rebirth
Propelling the vast, blind, rotating sky:
And, as the sun endows the moon with brightness,
Its light's refracted in the rainbow's storm,
So pain is in our tears; and in tears, beauty;
And beauty, joy. So all things are in all.

PERICLES So you are gone; feared father. (*Pause*) And he leaves
A gap that will be filled by vacancy.
'These things shall be my care.' What did Zeus
mean
In Homer?

ANAXAGORAS Herakleitos would say fire's
The origin of all things. For me, aither.
There must be other worlds, with fields and cities,
Plants—animals fixed firmly in the ground—
And sun and moon, as we have: for the moon
Is simply made of earth, with seas and cliffs;
The sun a red hot stone, larger than all
The Peloponnese. So, Pericles, remember,

Appearances are glimpses of what's hid;
And, as we know heart's cold by memory
Of sunny days, and thirst through loss of water;
The sea's salt by a spring's refreshing taste;
So each perception is achieved through pain.

PERICLES Old friend, from your far distant Klazomenai
Where the unending headlands wash the sea,
Your father long ago, with the Ionian
Army, burned the reed-thatched roofs of Sardis,
And lost his life striking the Persian throne.
Now mine, too, goes that journey we will tread
When our light fails. Leave me a while alone.

Exit ANAXAGORAS.

SCENE THREE

I'll lie down on my bed; or wash my hand
In the Aegean on a quiet strand.

PERICLES *dreams*.

XANTHIPPOS My older colleagues say your voice and bearing
Remind them strangely of Peisistratos,
Who brought the cult of Dionysus here
To Athens, and seduced the silly crowds
With festivals like the Panathenaea.
Your mother dreamed she gave a lion birth:
What would she think now if she trod the earth?

PERICLES Father! Father! I work long hours, and take
Responsible decisions; based—I hope—
On some religious view; and when I'm called
Will fall, hacked, fighting to save Athens' name!

XANTHIPPOS But your veins run with ideals, not with blood.
Could you do what I did to Artaÿctes
When Sestos was reduced to eating straps—
The leather thongs that stretched their nightly beds?

PERICLES Father, no. Nor would want to.

XANTHIPPOS Your good brother
Fought in my trireme first at Salamis,
While you, who'd gone ahead in the safe galleys
From sacked and burning Athens, wept your dog.

PERICLES Our dog stood, waiting, by the galley's side;
Then followed, swimming far across the strait,
And when he reached our warm and resting sand
Died, as I lifted him.

Exit XANTHIPPOS. *Enter* PINDAR.

PINDAR Man's life is just one day; now here, now gone—
A shadow's dream: but when this darkness falls,
A strong sun shines for them below, where fields
Of golden fruit and scarlet roses gleam
Through the bright incense at the immortal walls.

PERICLES But Pindar! Are we judged?

PINDAR In Acheron
Wise Rhadamanthys will not bless a lie.

PINDAR *fades*. *Enter* ANAXAGORAS.

ANAXAGORAS That's myth and nonsense. Our earth's flat in shape,
Though filled with hollow water, which spills seas,
And it is held suspended, lifted, by
That strongest of all things, almighty air.

ANAXAGORAS *fades*. *Enter* SOPHOCLES.

PERICLES But Sophocles, what of the African?

SOPHOCLES In every way, these things, they are ordained.

SOPHOCLES *fades*. *Enter* KALLIAS.

PERICLES Kallias!

KALLIAS The secrets at Eleusis teach
Our body is the prison of the soul.
Demeter, grieving for Persephone,
Let earth fall barren in her winter grief,
Searching the world—could not be comforted.
Eleusis' king gave her his roof, where she,
Holding his baby son in the hearth's flames
To purge it of its young mortality,
Was forced to reveal her name. She gave these rites;
In penance sent the child Triptolemos
Across the world to teach mankind how corn
Can grow, and that the secret seed must die
Before kind spring can wheaten waving gold.

KALLIAS *fades. Enter* XANTHIPPOS.

XANTHIPPOS Nailed him to a plank . . . (*Fades*)

PERICLES (*Wakes. Screams*) Aspasia!

SCENE FOUR

Enter ELPINIKE *veiled.*

PERICLES Who is that draped in half light? Yes? Come in.
Are you alone?

ELPINIKE I am.

PERICLES Come. Lift your veil
So I know who you are. Elpinike!
Aren't you a little old for games like this?
Besides, my father has just died, and my
Emotion's like a full moon spilled at sea.

ELPINIKE Life and shadow are intermingled, dappled:
I did not know. I'm sorry.

PERICLES Real death!
And loss of time that cannot be redeemed!

ELPINIKE There'll be a full state funeral?

PERICLES Who knows?
Yes. I suppose so; as to ritualize
Something preserves its sentiment, and makes
A spur to future action.

ELPINIKE Pericles,
I did not come to intrude. My youth's gone:
Part of the wonder was its evanescence.
I do not use a mirror any more.
No. I have come to plead for your restraint
When you indict my brother Kimon.

PERICLES Yes,
He is for trial. So—I lay the charge?

ELPINIKE The Democrats vote that you make a speech
In prosecution. There'll be others, too.
Haven't you fought as colleagues, and lost friends
In camps and anguish I could never guess?

PERICLES We've watched the snails climb spongy wrecks together,
And cooked a meal upon a distant shore.

ELPINIKE You know he would not take bribes.

PERICLES Yes, I know.

ELPINIKE He lacks the statesman's necessary instinct
For flexibility and compromise.

PERICLES He has great charm . . .

ELPINIKE And reputation, too.

PERICLES Ambition-grown acclaim turns into virtue,
And reputation is the name we use.

ELPINIKE All Athens knows that though the far horizon
Of most men's eyes may reach our city's wall,
Your own is lifted to an Empire's greatness . . .

PERICLES Empire?

ELPINIKE So Kimon says. Democracy
Cannot sustain a lengthy war. The crowd
Will change its sympathies like cream to butter
Turned rancid with the casualty lists.
Why are you with the rabble, not with him?

PERICLES These are not matters for a woman. Leave me.
I know your thoughts. I promise nothing. He
And Ephialtes split the city now.
No one need know you've come alone. Brave sister,
Now go. An owl calls to its quavering mate;
Mist presses all the night scents to the ground:
Our feet are damp. Euangelos! Wake, boy.
Take a bright torch and see this lady home.

Fade to black after EUANGELOS *and* ELPINIKE *have left.*

SCENE FIVE

KLEINIAS Please would you draw that cord around the meeting?
Yes; give us space, but not too much. The crowd
Must clearly hear whatever we decide,
Especially as Kimon is on trial.
Citizens! Resident aliens! And all!
You know the constitution of our Athens,
Formed first by Solon, shaped by Kleisthenes
(And—may I say—my father [most of you
Are too young to remember]

FIRST CITIZEN All of us
Are over thirty, or we can't be here!

KLEINIAS Yes, yes; but (*Indicating audience*) in the agora they're not.
My father Alkibiades fought with
Kleisthenes in our revolution's wars.)
Well. Kleisthenes Alkmaeonid laid down
All power now rests in the people's hands.

CROWD (*Shout*) Yes!

KLEINIAS With the Assembly of the Sovereign People!

CROWD (*Shout*) Yes!

KLEINIAS Here in the market we today are one
Of two subordinates: the Boule (or Council),
The other's (*Pointing up*) on the Areopagus.
All of us in the Council are elected,
Chosen by lot for office for one year,
The Chairman for one day—sunset to sunset.
That's why you find a soldier now presiding:
Your Kleinias.

SECOND CITIZEN Hurrah!

FIRST CITIZEN Get on with it!

KLEINIAS Kimon, whose daring, blood and treasure put
All southern Asia into Athens' hands
At Eurymedon; Kimon, who planted paths
And sheltered gardens for the learning young;
Kimon, who gave these plane-trees in our market
That shield us from this early morning sun;
Kimon, of the Conservative ruling party,
Founder of the Strymon colony;
Kimon the General, son of Miltiades
Victor of Marathon, is now arraigned.
Where is the prosecution's spokesman?

EPHIALTES Here.

KLEINIAS Ephialtes, Leader of the Opposition:
Aware that if your charge is frivolous,
And gains less than one fifth of all the votes,
You will be fined one thousand drachmas—speak!

EPHIALTES Kimon has failed to found the colony;
Cheated our trust. He broke rebelling Thasos:
But did you know Thasos asked Sparta's help?
And Kimon, as you all know, loves his Sparta:

He calls his son Lakedaimonios.
Kimon had our great army—each of you saw it
Sailing into the East, while at Piraeus
The jetties and the cheering eyes kissed off
Excited tears, and shouldered children's waves
Disturbed high gnats and filled the trireme sails.
With such a force he could (you know our fighters!)
In Macedonia have conquered all.
What held him back? Why was that wheat of Athens
Harvested—murdered—by barbarian knives?
Our widows, and our orphans on the roadsides,
Know that I tell the truth. Was it because
King Alexander of rich Macedon
Bribed him? Yes; Kimon's proud and generous,
Yet not so long ago—do you remember?—
He was near-bankrupt, beggared by the fine
We people rightly laid upon his father.
When he had failed to liberate our isles
With a great fleet. The father hatched the son;
And the son, too, has soiled the people's trust,
Whose loved ones rot now in the mud of death.
Citizens, jurors: I propose to you
Banishment from our city, with a fine,
Fangs our own throat. Themistocles—remember,
We gently banished?—fights for Persia's king!
He has betrayed the city. Now, let Athens
Propose the only penalty: his death.

CROWD *Hubbub: mixed reception.*

KLEINIAS (*Trying to make himself heard*) It is forbidden under pain of death
(*Silence restored*) To quote law falsely while within this court;
So I will not. I'll merely say, in passing,
That punishment's for traitors. Pericles:
I am informed you will complete the case.

PERICLES I am elected by the prosecution
To second Ephialtes.

KLEINIAS Well; go on!

PERICLES
Kimon was my commanding officer,
And none of us must be in any doubt:
He is an eagle in a sky of hawks.
His lands, it's true, were mortgaged. Since, he has
Unfenced his orchards. All may wander there
And crop their mouths' delight. His home is used,
Often, for Council meetings of this Boule.
Each day his kitchen door feeds freely all
Those with no sandals who know misery.
His servants change rich clothes with passers-by,
Turning each brown grub to a butterfly
Who laughs with coin. Where does this money grow?
I do not say he's bribed: but we must know.

KLEINIAS
That all?

PERICLES
Kimon is popular with allies
Because he does not press them to supply
Fighters and triremes any more; just cash.
Please will he tell us where that tribute goes?

KLEINIAS
Finished?

PERICLES
Yes.

KLEINIAS
Now, Kimon. What have you to answer them?
Remember: the death penalty is asked.

KIMON
Were it not true that many men have died—
Not through my fault—this would be farcical.
All tribute goes to Delos, not to me,
Where it is held in the League's treasury.
Many Ionian and Thessalian states
Have flashed their ransom in our conquering sun
Begging me to be proxenos at Athens
For them, with a mine's womb scraped. I've refused.
Only for Sparta, who pays nothing, am I
Official proxenos. Them I admire.
Their moderation and simplicity
We all should honour, as an elder brother

Who sets example. As for what I own:
It is well known great Kallias the Wealthy
Paid off my father's fine. He married, too,
My sister, dowerless—Elpinike:
For which I, here in Athens' agora,
Publicly thank him from my inmost soul.

CROWD (*Cheers*)

KIMON Now, to the charge of leading men to slaughter.
Here are the facts. We fought for, and controlled
The city called Nine Ways, and scattered all
Edonians who still remained like ants
From scalding water.

CROWD (*Cheers*)

KIMON There we wedged our camp—
We had a colony half built for us!
I gave strict orders to consolidate
And fly no rash adventures; but Leagros,
Holding Defence Command, was struck by hubris.
He led a column out, while I at sea
Tended the fleet; pushed inland to Drabescus
With no rearguard support; was cut off, ambushed,
And all our men were slaughtered and beheaded:
Edonians and Thracians lit the pyres.
For them I weep as much as any man.
They were my soldiers; known and loved by me.

KLEINIAS Each member citizen take up one shell
And let it fall into one of these jars:
This side if you think Kimon is at fault;
This, if he's won his freedom. Vote begin!

ETERAPOULA (*Watching*) They're jealous of his geniality.

ASPASIA If that physique and strength's condemned to die
We'll leave for Sparta, where girls are outspoken . . .

PERICHORE Spartans have marriage customs we should try.

They shut the unmarried young in a dark room
With straw and vine leaves—girls wear scented plants—
And first blind catch is bedded, wedded, home.

ETERAPOULA As good a lottery as ours: or this!

KLEINIAS Kimon's acquitted! Ephialtes, you
Are fined one thousand drachmas. (*Wild cheering*) Hear me speak!
The law entitles Kimon the last word.

CROWD Speech! Speech! Speech! Speech! Speech!

KIMON Thank you. Thank all of you. Your music deafens!
I never learned to play the instruments
Myself, or sing. All I know how to do
Is make a city enviably great. (*Cheers*)
First, I shall pay off Ephialtes' fine:
He's poor, has no estates—and needs a friend!
Next, I announce Thukydides elected
New leader of our Party. Last, the news
Is a great earthquake has destroyed the Spartan
Capital. There are just five houses left.

FIRST CITIZEN They don't know how to build.

SECOND CITIZEN Could it come here?

KIMON King Archidamos saved the citizens
By sounding the war trumpet. At that bray
All Spartans take their weapons, leave their homes,
And gather round the king; so most were saved.
Their Helots have rebelled, and in the chaos
On Mount Ithome make a fortress nest.
The Spartans ask our help.

EPHIALTES We must not send it!
Sparta cares nothing for democracy.
The Helots fight for freedom!

KLEINIAS Silence, you

Ungrateful man! Pericles, should you side
With such a party that can flower this cactus?

PERICLES If we send democratic Athens' soldiers,
Sparta will owe us much. She will hear, too,
(For who can stop a soldier bragging?) how
All citizens, from high to low, control
Our city's destiny in speaking trust.

KIMON Have I your sanction for one third the army?
Up to four thousand hoplites? Volunteers?
Would you let mighty Greece and the Aegean
Stumble with one leg lame, when we, the other,
Can muscle help?

CROWD Kimon, go! Take the troops!

KLEINIAS Passed overwhelmingly! We shall miss you.
Come! The Assembly now has much to do.

PERICLES Events, like ever-changing skies, demand
That we adapt and, deer-like, stay alert.
Come, Ephialtes; watch. Let Kimon stray.
With Sparta crippled, we may have our way.

SCENE SIX

PERICLES Anaxagoras, are you relieved?

ANAXAGORAS I don't know what to think. That was the worst
I've ever heard you speak.

PERICLES Frog in my throat—
Lumpy toad, rather. Look, you white-haired Mind!
Don't you see opportunity gape open,
Now Kimon's gone, our city jumping with
The cold fear of a fish whose dinner's hooked?
They dare not vote against the ruling party,
And only those who seldom have to work
Make up the juries. Say we pay each juror
With coin spilled high from sale of spoils of war?
Never has Athens been as rich, or restless.

We can afford, say, two obols a day.
Then feared dependence on the hand and favour
Of archons on the Areopagus
Will loosen. Shall we try it?

ANAXAGORAS There are seeds here;
Seeds of all shapes and colours, which in time
May come to being. Our weak senses cannot
Predict all that might be.

PERICLES You say man's hands
Make him the wisest of all living things?
Let's grasp this opportunity and try!

Enter EPHIALTES.

ANAXAGORAS Come! You spoke well. Your colleague has a plan
To pay the jurors; buy their hearts from Kimon . . .

EPHIALTES 'Bribing the people with the public funds'
As Damon says. Pericles, now's the time
For our assault on Areopagus.
We'll strip it of all powers . . .

PERICLES Except for those
For trying murder, which have a religious
Basis, and would not be popular.

EPHIALTES Remove its jurisdiction over laws
Where now it reigns the supreme arbiter
High on that naked hill where pupils shrink
To look. Then its cold grasp that holds us back
From change will slacken.

ANAXAGORAS Make it a murder court
And nothing more.

PERICLES Democracy can then
Truly reach up to feel the future's pulse.
Athens will be an education to
All Greece. Who knows? Beyond!

EPHIALTES Those grim pro-Spartan
(*To* PERICLES) (Forgive me) unelected aristocrats
Will lose their emblem of authority,
And wither by the unleashed, running power
Of our new racing votes.

PERICLES Till a new balance
Between all individual citizens
And the just interests of the State hangs, hovers,
In ever-changing equilibrium.
Go; make that speech.

Exit EPHIALTES.

SCENE SEVEN

Enter SOPHOCLES.

SOPHOCLES The Furies who still live beneath that hill
Have found a poet's voice in Aeschylus.
The Chorus of his latest play cries out
Conquered by great Athene's casting vote:
'The old is trodden by the fresh, and vengeance
Nurtures my heart to creep on blighted plant
And child plague-poisoned. Athens shall learn to weep
The folly of her reckless sacrilege.'

PERICLES Aeschylus is too old to change. How does
The play close?

SOPHOCLES With a plea for peace; a fear
Of civil war; prayer; hope for our city—
Provided those who leave the rocky hill,
Honoured, find home on the Acropolis.

ANAXAGORAS Will Ephialtes let them?

Enter EPHIALTES.

EPHIALTES We have won!
All we had hoped for has been voted through!

ANAXAGORAS The Areopagus is stripped of power!

PERICLES You time it well, while Kimon is eclipsed.
The crowd call you to tread the balcony
And hear their wine-breath.

EPHIALTES This is my greatest
Day. If I should live a thousand years,
This part we've played just now in Athens' history
Will be my height of noon.

PERICLES You have the freedom,
A clear hand now, to drive on, transform Athens.
The last, archaic stumbling-rein is slipped.
Statecraft gives place to stagecraft now; go out
Accept acclaim.

EPHIALTES You too!

PERICLES This day is yours.

EPHIALTES *steps out on to balcony to shouting crowd.*

EPHIALTES When you elected me as General,
In spite of Kimon's arch-Conservatives,
I swore that, uncorrupted, unafraid,
I'd serve you all; (*Cheers*) the people; (*Cheers*) you alone.
Not old, high masters. (*Cheers*) On the open seas
We found no enemies; so here at home
Your battles I have fought. To pledge you all
And celebrate this hinge of history
I pour you here the heady, unmixed draught
Of freedom! (*Cheers*) Let me bring Pericles to you.
He has supported, guided, helped, encouraged
His first of equals. Never hold his name,
His class against him. He's the people's friend!

PERICLES *joins* EPHIALTES *to cheers.*

PERICLES To Ephialtes our established leader—
Now the First Minister in Athens, give

The laurel crown planted by Kleisthenes.
News has arrived that Sparta has turned back
Our hoplites. They've rejected Kimon, too.
Our offered hand of friendship's knocked aside
In boorish mistrust and crass insolence,

CROWD *angry*.

Because, no doubt, they fear Athenian soldiers,
Men like ourselves, may feed the Helots' hope,
And Sparta turn into democracy.

EPHIALTES I said they should not go. Now Kimon swears
He will rescind, undo, all we've achieved,
And put the death-long, greybeard sinecures,
Who held us down, back where they blot the sun!

FIRST CITIZEN Ostracize, kick him out!

SECOND CITIZEN Ostracize Kimon!

PERICLES (*To* EPHIALTES) In Sparta Kimon is too democratic;
In Athens not enough. Yes, he must go
Or worse may drain him. Civil war could burst
The racing fever of this city's tossing.
A ten-year poultice is not merciless.

EPHIALTES (*To* CROWD) Will you vote now? To send Kimon to exile?

PERICLES (*To* EPHIALTES) This time for saving the Athenian lives!

EPHIALTES The vote must be unanimous. Shall we
Test your ability to keep what's gained?

CROWD Vote! Vote! Ostracize Kimon. Vote!

EPHIALTES I will, then: as your leader, ask you all
Aloud if Kimon's to be ostracized?

CROWD (*Loud shout*) Yes!

EPHIALTES Now call if he is to be welcomed home.

CROWD (*Silent*)

EPHIALTES Kimon has gone! (*Wild applause*) Send messengers. Clerks! Write it
Exactly as it's happened.

PERICLES (*Aside to* EPHIALTES) His virtues are
His downfall. We may need them. (*To* CROWD) Megara calls
For help in war with Corinth. Sparta's left her.
Will you allow our General, Ephialtes,
To take returning hoplites to their aid?

FIRST CITIZEN (*Aside*) That's a first step to war with Sparta!

CROWD Yes!

A dagger is thrown up from the crowd. EPHIALTES *is seen to have a bloody dagger in him; he falls.*

PERICLES Who threw the dagger? Catch him! Down there! Run!
(*Pause*) Your leader has been killed. His day of triumph
Becomes his last. His freedom has been won.
Go to your homes. The expert assassin's held.

A scratched shard is thrown or passed up to him, which he reads.

'Aristodicus, a Boiotian thug'
With a soul like black crystal. Please stay in
Tonight. There may be violence on the streets.
Go. Go.

SCENE EIGHT

SOPHOCLES
Pericles; you need help.
With Kimon gone and Ephialtes dead,
You are the sole inheritor of Athens;
Her nurse in grief—but all her hope's in you.

PERICLES
If individuals had been different
The circumstances would not be the same.
The range of our emotions beggars language:
All are beyond expressing. Joy and grief
Are words that narrow their infinity.

KALLIAS
What can I say to sweeten your dark cup,
Except that Persia has at last agreed
Our treaty.

PERICLES
Well done. What are the final terms?

KALLIAS
We keep the Aegean and the Eastern cities,
And leave him Cyprus, Egypt and beyond.
Now peace is ours in perpetuity
With Persia. I signed. Our fleet's sailing home.

ANAXAGORAS
The tribute-treasure has arrived in Athens
From sacred Delos island for safe-keeping.
But now the Persian threat has passed . . .?

PERICLES
It stays here.

KLEINIAS
Sparta has turned down Athens' invitation
We scattered to all Greek states, to send good men
Here to discuss rebuilding temples which
Barbarian Persia burned; and future plans
For tight security on our high seas!

PERICLES
Did any state reply?

KLEINIAS
Not even one.

PERICLES
The Great Panathenaea festival
Comes round next year. We'll make that take its place;
Rebuild our temples on our own, with tribute:
Giving, for the returning trireme thousands,

Employment, with ideals as well as pay.
Leave me a little free from cares of state.
My colleague lies there. Sophocles?

SOPHOCLES My friend?

PERICLES As the unresting, swift and turning swallow
Finds its companion hawked out of the sky
In sudden shriek, yet it flies on the wind's wings,
On into safety, spared—and gratitude,
Relief, sick dread, and sadness blend and prism—
So I, who only see our city's future
Through this assassination's tears, need time
To grieve the violence that brought his end.

SOPHOCLES But swallows bring new springtime. Athens lies
Frightened, in your cupped hands. What you believe
She will become. They know that you are wise
And, for a while, will trust what you conceive.
Arrow your grief to splendour, and create
An Athens all the world will imitate.

END OF ACT TWO

Act Three

SCENE ONE

The Acropolis. Great Panathenaea.

EURIPIDES Pericles has a son!

SOPHOCLES Aspasia's tree,
Euripides, has borne fruit. May it be (*Pointing up*)
That peaceful olive at the gable's centre,
Between Poseidon and Athene, where
Sun's rays catch Zeus's thunderbolt in gold.
Pheidias breeds our new world from the old:
The gods, and men who fell at Marathon,
Centaurs, and giants, and the sack of Troy.
He's dressed the Amazons in Persian clothes!
Surely the Trojans are the parallel?

EURIPIDES Fame, and the Eastern crown with all its treasures,
And all that grasping power and theft may win—
What are their flashing piles of rubied spoil
Compared to youth? I have no wish to live
If the sweet graces of fulfilled desire
Married to sculpture's living poetry,
Music and every art, desert my pulse.

SOPHOCLES When passions weaken, we may find release
From prison where a madman is the gaoler.
Love woven through with wisdom is the gift
Of old age. You're right: chisels of Pheidias
Transmute the stories of our race through stone.

EURIPIDES He's given it contemporary themes,
And dared to mix our market with the gods!
All the Olympians are there, but so

Is our procession (*Enter* PERICLES), with the
water-jars,
The chariots, and cows, Athene's robe
The sail, the cavalcade . . .

PERICLES Athens at worship:
Both civic and religious—every man
And woman leading lives of celebration.
We must not fall short of our fathers' gifts
To us, but passionately love our city.
Pheidias and Iktinos have created
Beauty that marvels injuries of time
Into a freshness wet with living spirit
Touching each stone with such unfading youth
Our souls, made evergreen, become divine.

SCENE TWO

Enter THUKYDIDES.

THUKYDIDES I've fought you every inch the way on this,
Pericles . . .

PERICLES Yes, you have, Thukydides.

THUKYDIDES And shall do. You've dressed Athens like a harlot
With contributions pulled by trireme force
From those who were our allies. The excuse
Was, we'd protect them from the Persian galleys;
Delos would be impartial treasurer.
Now Persia's peace is signed, and Delos stripped.
Where does the tribute come? To busy Athens.
From whom? Our rich in far Greek cities. Why?
So you can pander to the idle loungers,
And win their comfortable workers' votes.
You pay their training in the fleet, send them
To colonies of easy merchandise—
Over five thousand planted by you abroad
On land that was not ours . . .

SOPHOCLES It's not so simple,

Thukydides. You've never fought in battle;
Only in Council's world of fair debate.

THUKYDIDES I'm brother-in-law to our lamented Kimon,
Who—right to the end—fought for our Eastern
sails.

PERICLES (*To* SOPHOCLES) We know, all of us, you have done
far greater,
Braver, cleverer things than he has, but
This is his moment, Sophocles. Let him speak.

THUKYDIDES You *are* an aristocrat; you patronizing
Turncoat.

PERICLES I'm a radical at home:
That's wrong, you say. Yet, when I check the few
Revolting allies you say that's wrong too!

THUKYDIDES The world's gone mad. The rich turn radical,
While the poor lift their voices against change.

PERICLES The country folk hate change. Their crop and
donkey
Are all the bent back they have to survive,
But in the city our poor cry for bread,
For which they'll work. We must feed them, or fall.

THUKYDIDES Look at the marble dust that clouds the houses,
Filling our lungs, and drying back our throats!
Look at the noise and chaos all your soldiers
Home from the wars could cause, and do! Far
worse,
The name of Athens, once so loved, is feared,
Dishonoured; and, with precious stones and statues,
You flaunt these crimes on the Acropolis!

PERICLES All that you see in gold could, *in extremis*,
Be taken off and melted down. Meanwhile,
It hangs in beauty. Do your own life-savings
Win love? Provided we defend our allies—
Which we have done, and will (sprawling Piraeus,

The port of Athens you so hate, ensures that)—
Then how we use the tribute is our business.
We give our lives. Not one horse, one ship, soldier,
Or seaman do most of them send: just coin.

SOPHOCLES What we see here will lift to inspiration
And noble thoughts all hearts throughout the isles.

THUKYDIDES What you have made is an imperial city
Based on dishonest, ruthless, sudden peace.

PERICLES In this compelling fiction laced with truth
You undermine all that we have achieved.
Tomorrow we'll debate in the Assembly,
And I shall challenge you to ostracize.

Exit THUKYDIDES.

EURIPIDES Pericles; was that wise?

PERICLES Well, time will show.
This city cannot hold us both, and grow.

SCENE THREE

ASPASIA I've fed the chickens, but they peck each other
Till their rear feathers scatter and bleed raw!
Will they give eggs, or should we kill and pluck them?

PERICLES Why, give them time, and see.

ASPASIA Ah, Pericles!
Time is the enemy, you say, for you.
For me it hangs in dusty swathes across
The windows of my thoughts till you return
And play with our small baby, and with me.

PERICLES You make the rocks of Etna melt. Those days
And nights we are together feed my strength
Like the young sun waking a sparkling sea

As it climbs up the sky like a fresh bridegroom
Ready to race and challenge earth's delights,
Then arcs to you, sweeter than honeycomb
Still hummed with bees; his circuit won, sinks spilled
Into the western foam.

ASPASIA Here; hold your son
Who has your name.

PERICLES Poor boy!

ASPASIA But not your world.
Why did you make that new law, limiting
Citizenship only to those whose parents
On both sides were Athenians already?

PERICLES Immigrants pour into our city, drawn
By power, certainty of work to do,
Payment of casual civil posts—like juries,
And knowledge that, if they should die in war,
The State will care for wife and children.

ASPASIA Couldn't
You wait until our baby was secure?

PERICLES Grain has arrived from Egypt, a free gift
From Psammetichos, whose brave father died
Crucified at the hands of Queen Amestris,
The Great King's mother—breaking safe-conduct's
oath!
This corn has been distributed to all
Citizens freely—fourteen thousand. But
Five thousand more tried, who don't qualify.

ASPASIA Themistocles and Kimon were the sons
Of alien mothers! Is democracy
Shrinking from its famed generosity
To treat all equal?

PERICLES In this case the gift
Will cause bad feeling—which is what we want:
To stop the Assembly sending troops to Egypt

In thanks, breaking the peace of Kallias.

ASPASIA You have discouraged marriage to foreigners,
But what of all our colonies abroad?
Is celibacy now to be encouraged
Like weary sun on winter afternoons?
In spite of local pride's designs and foundries
Throughout the islands and the subject towns,
You have imposed Athenian weights and coinage!
Your silver owl brings hatred. Did you know
That Anaxagoras will be impeached?
It's not him they're attacking: it is you.

PERICLES Tomorrow I will gamble all. Athene
On the Acropolis holds high men's hopes.
If I win, the Conservatives are broken:
And if I lose? There is a world beyond.

SCENE FOUR

ETERAPOULA *painting pottery*. PERICHORE *weaving*.

PERICHORE What are you painting on fired earth?

ETERAPOULA A bird.

PERICHORE An owl? As I was coming home just now
From the procession, a small owl crunched beetles
That came into our torchlight.

ETERAPOULA How I wish
The streets were not so narrow and so dark!

PERICHORE Those empty workshops and unfinished houses!
I ran the last lanes from the Agora.

ETERAPOULA Men are such pests!

PERICHORE Do owls really milk goats?

ETERAPOULA They use a bat's heart to clean out their nest
Of ants.

PERICHORE A bat's heart! I want a nightingale
Here as my pet in a clean cage.

ETERAPOULA Well, buy one!
Penelope had twenty geese as pets.

PERICHORE Penelope! Well, look; I'm weaving, too.
When I was seven, I carried a water-jug
At the procession; stringed figs round my neck.
I held a basket . . .

ETERAPOULA You never wove the sail,
The peplos of Athene; never will.
You must be rich, a virgin (under eleven—
They play for safety), and high class, for that.

PERICHORE It's only festivals and funerals
That take us out for fun.

ETERAPOULA The theatre?

PERICHORE When we can afford it, or be taken.

ETERAPOULA Didn't you know Pericles makes the state
Pay for our seats now? Is that buying votes?
At that last play of Aeschylus, about
The furies, two fat girls miscarried!

PERICHORE Well,
What do you think of this Euripides?

ETERAPOULA He hates us women!

PERICHORE Yes: he has two wives.

ETERAPOULA 'No home should have a woman cleverer
Or more perceptive than her husband. Take
A stupid woman, not a scheming luster.'

PERICHORE What horrid things he says! Are women lustful?

ETERAPOULA Nine times as much as men, Teiresias

Tells us; the silly ex-hermaphrodite.
The sound of children playing before bedtime
Drains the last light. I can't see any more.
Do you like it? (*Holds up her piece of pottery*)

PERICHORE A cock-fight! A love-token!

ETERAPOULA Themistocles set them as men's example:
'They endure pain, not for their gods, or country,
But simply to avoid defeat.'

Enter ASPASIA.

ASPASIA Come girls.
The sky grows violet and bees fly home.
I've been with Pericles, who's full of cares:
Elpinike's divorced from Kallias . . .

ETERAPOULA She's not! Why?

ASPASIA Zeus knows: and a band of exiles
From Athens has control of Chaironeia.
Tolmides wants a small force taken out
Led by himself and Kleinias: volunteers.
Pericles is against: advises caution.

PERICHORE I like that last decree of Kleinias
About each city sending a festal cow!

ASPASIA It was about punishment for failed tribute.
This empire's growing sullen. Here at home
Jealous Hermippos comics up his plays
Portraying me—us. Get some rest. Storm rain!
No men will come. They're drunk with blood again.

Sounds of heavy rain. Fade to black.

SCENE FIVE

DIOPEITHES Bring in the omen. See it, everyone?
This ram's head has one single horn. I ask
Lampon the Seer, and Anaxagoras,
To show its meaning to us.

LAMPON Diopeithes,
I shall. This city's split between two parties
At fever pitch. The rich Conservatives
Who want the green ways back. When Kimon lived,
The noblemen and farmers were at one,
The poor gave thanks for generosity,
And the Long Walls did not enclose a mob
Of seaport hangers-on and immigrants.
Thukydides, son of Pindar's old friend
The wrestling trainer tall Melesias,
Brother-in-law of the late Kimon, leads.
Against him, Alkmaeonid Pericles—
To whom the Empire and democracy
And the great building programme of long walls
Down to Piraeus, and the Parthenon,
And everywhere, are dowelled and iron-clamped,
Mortised, inseparable. This portent
Signifies there will be one horn of state,
Not two, after today.

DIOPEITHES Anaxagoras?

ANAXAGORAS Bring me an axe. (*Cuts it in half*) Just as I thought. The brain's
Deformed, and has contracted like an egg
To force one horn out. Simple natural cause.

CROWD *Cheers, and also cries of* 'Shame!'

DIOPEITHES There's a decree we've passed: that those who teach
Impiety, do not believe in gods,
Deny the sun and moon divinity,
Will be impeached. Now, Anaxagoras;
Can you defend yourself against the charge.
(*Venomously*) You are an atheist?

PERICLES This is not right!
The city comes to settle, once for all,
Which way her future lies. (CROWD *support for* PERICLES)

EURIPIDES They are both right:
One shows the cause, the other sees the meaning.

DIOPEITHES Thukydides. Is there more you would say?

THUKYDIDES You've heard me speak of the vote-catching bribes,
The colonies planted to instil fear
Among the allies, lest they should default
Or withdraw from what was the Delian League
But now is Athens' empire. The Defence Fund
Is wasted on the artists and the stones
That gild and litter our austere, our moderate
City, as it was. These Long Walls hold
A sprawling urban population safe;
But are the farms of Attica secure?
No! The imperial policy is urban,
Immigrant-based, disruptive; insolent
To us at home, to our friends overseas;
And morally corrupt: fills idlers' pockets,
And makes the rich redundant. Even now
Our wealthy exiles have won Chaironeia,
And Tolmides and Kleinias take troops
To shed our own blood on both sides. Pericles
Is the cause, the evil mind that's made
Athens a harlot like Aspasia!

PERICLES Look up, on the Acropolis! Is that
A harlot's home? Thukydides, I here
Denounce you by that very law invoked
To strike down Anaxagoras: impiety!
Thukydides calls Virgin Athene 'whore'!
The words are from his lips. Do we need more?

CROWD Ostracize Thukydides! Ostracize Thukydides!

DIOPEITHES Is that a formal call?

CROWD It is!

DIOPEITHES Who would defend him?

CROWD (*Silent*)

DIOPEITHES He's exiled!

CROWD (*Cheering*) Pericles!

SCENE SIX

DIOPEITHES
Before you leave this place,
There's one more charge of gross impiety.
(*Pause*) Pheidias! Call him in!

PERICLES
Pheidias!

DIOPEITHES
Come,
And stand here. Are your friends, associates,
A whore, Aspasia; and an atheist,
Anaxagoras? What? No reply?
Have you embezzled gold for your own use
Given to you for glorifying Athens?
Still no reply? Have you, in gross bad taste,
Mixed modern life with sacred truths of gods
On that bank vault on the Acropolis?
Impiety? Lastly, on the great shield
Of your vast statue in the Parthenon
There are two heads embossed: One of yourself,
And one of Pericles.

PERICLES
He has a speech
Impediment. May I speak for him?

DIOPEITHES
No.

CROWD Yes! Yes! Yes! Yes!

DIOPEITHES
Well, then.

PERICLES
What we have here is the ability
Of man's unbounded mind to be dragged on
Into believing, finding evidence
For things which could not possibly be true.
Could atheism and impiety
In a mind have created the Athene

Parthenos? Think of Olympia:
The superhuman majesty of Zeus?
That bronze Promachos thanks for Marathon
Whose distant spear, when lightning splits the sky,
Is seen beyond the cape at Sunium?
All of them fashioned by his mastery!
This answer must suffice:
(*An account book is passed to* PERICLES)
Not one gold ounce
Is unaccounted for. All can be stripped, and weighed.
If calumny is best repelled by facts,
Why, here they are! We have them—come and see!
Is he acquitted?

CROWD Yes!

DIOPEITHES Here! Who's in charge?

PERICLES You are: in this court.

DIOPEITHES I am.

SCENE SEVEN

Enter SOPHOCLES.

DIOPEITHES Sophocles?

SOPHOCLES As General, may I address you all?
Has the court finished?

DIOPEITHES Here I close the court.
Your news?

SOPHOCLES Both Kleinias and Tolmides
Have died in ambush on Mount Helicon.
Half our Athenian force is dead. The rest,
Five hundred, held as hostages.

PERICLES The price?

SOPHOCLES Athens renounces all claims on Boiotia.

PERICLES By a mere fragment of our army, all
Our continental power lost in one day.
But (*Pause*) we must bring our young men safely home.

SOPHOCLES As a result Euboia has rebelled.

PERICLES Do you agree, all Athens gathered here,
We bring the ransomed home? But I myself,
With a full army, equipped and well supported,
Move swiftly to crush any further threat?

CROWD (*Cries of full support*)

SECOND CITIZEN You were right not to back their expedition!

FIRST CITIZEN With more support they might have won—

PERICLES Or lost
More lives in those forest ravines, so ripe
For ambush!

FIRST CITIZEN Take the fleet this time!

PERICLES I will.
Euboia must be reined and brought to heel.

SCENE EIGHT

The scene begins with EURIPIDES *alone in the theatre.*

EURIPIDES I throw a stone along the waves and it catches and lifts the air
Like a fawn escaped from hunters, new leapt from the cutting snare
Free at last in a meadow of loosestrife and hyacinth,
Out of reach of the dogs' teeth through the tree-woven labyrinth
Of panting, wild-eyed panic that strained each muscle hard,
Out in exultant freedom now with head-high disregard
Of anything other than living he races the riverside,
Far from the sound of mankind, where the woodland animals hide.
On now faster than falcon, with the wind for aching friend,
He finds the blessing of forest where shade and safety blend.

KALLIAS Euripides; here in this open-air
Theatre I can hear each word you say
Right at the back. Whatever are you doing?

EURIPIDES Playing a playwright rehearsing a rehearsal.
As Pericles' Odeion is kept locked up
Because the masts that fought at Salamis,
The woodwork, people splinter as souvenirs,
So I shout here while nobody's about.
Kallias, your name's on everybody's lips:
The Aphrodite statue Kalamis
Has built on the Acropolis to you
As peacemaker with Persia; and—of course—
Your divorce from painted Elpinike.

KALLIAS Painted? Oh, you mean on the Stoa wall
Where Polygnotos (one of her many lovers)
Gave her face in a picture to Ladike—
Amasis' wife who, if she could not make

Him consummate their marriage, was to die.
Sardonic compliment.

EURIPIDES Now I see why
Your statue is of Aphrodite! Athens
Is proud of open speech and freedom's laws.
Cities who're ruled behind closed doors at dusk
Look pallid, shifty. In our open day
Elpinike's affairs make gossip gay.

Enter PINDAR.

Pindar! Kallias here's immortalized
In bronze. Are you to sing his ode?

PINDAR My friends,
I'm here to visit Athens and Aegina
Once more before I dress my limbs in clay.

KALLIAS Not yet; but welcome! Your Thebes now has back
Its oligarchs, since Kleinias was ambushed—
And is it true they've fined you heavily
For praising Athens?

EURIPIDES What barbarians!

PINDAR Yes, they have. But the bronze Pheidias cast
Of gods and heroes with Miltiades
At Delphi still remains there undefaced.

KALLIAS That vaulting praise of Athens? Pindar, we
Will pay you double from our public funds
For your immortal fine. Here, Pheidias
Nearly completes the harmonizing vision
Pericles dreams, that all of Hellas can
Unite in worship: Athens, Sparta too;
And so both Dorian and Ionian styles
Blend in the Parthenon.

EURIPIDES Sparta? Ugh!
They're the antithesis of all we love.
We've settled their lost Helots at Naupaktos

Opposite them on the Corinthian Gulf,
And now they say we've done it to provoke!
They're jealous, and just want a cause for war.

Enter SOPHOCLES.

Sophocles! You are Chairman of the Board
Of the League Treasury, all the gold stored
In high Athene's temple. Pericles
Must find that most convenient. This year
All contributions will be reassessed!
What is the battle news, great General?

SOPHOCLES As sweet as summer and as sad as grief.
Pericles crushed rebellion in Euboia.
Drove out the population from one town
That massacred a trireme: in their place,
He gives their homes and land to just one thousand
Athenian families as rich reward.
That is the summer. Now for worse. Megara
Has turned on us. We built their long walls for them
Before we built ours: from the town to sea.
They used them—cut to death our garrison.
Andokides—(*To* EURIPIDES) and your friend
Socrates—
Have fought their way back through the shepherds'
paths
To warn us Sparta's army's on the march.

PINDAR Against us? No. Surely, to strip away
The Phokians from Delphi, and demand
Sparta has first right to the oracle:
They've carved that on the head of the bronze wolf.

KALLIAS The Phokians are our allies.

EURIPIDES (*Having listened to a whispered message from a boy runner*)
Here's more news:
Sparta's young king Pleistoanax leads them.
They've swept the cornfields of Eleusis clean,
And near the hills that look down on the vines
And olives of our plain of Athens wait.

This is a land no army has subdued,
Serene and delicate in its pure air
Where Aphrodite trails her fingers in
Our river Kephisos, so that the wind
At evening gently fills the air with longing,
And all the arts and Muses find their home.
How can they sacrilege an honoured truce?

SOPHOCLES Kolonos and my home are all that stand
Between us. Horse-cropped soil and nightingales.
The loveliest land I know. I'll gladly die there.

PINDAR Aeschylus is dead: in distant Sicily
By a strange accident.

KALLIAS Our Aeschylus?

EURIPIDES His ivy and his sacred pine, his dances
Over the mountain-side at dawn, his earthquake,
His protean god, now lion, snake, now bull;
And that great power which can bring back youth—
All I have stolen from him, I return
In admiration and humility.

Enter PERICLES.

If we are now to fight, who knows if death
Is not full life? And our life here true death?
We only know that all who feel the sun
Are full of grief and sickness. Those who've gone
Are never touched by such things any more.

PERICLES The enemy's not death, but cynicism:
Disinclination to become involved.
We have created in our single city
The noblest system ever known to man,
Where every citizen has self-respect,
And some control over his city's life.
This glory we've achieved, with its superb
And sublime confidence and certainty
That now controls an Empire one thousand times
And more its size, depends on self-belief;

A clear eye on the future; and a courage
That will fight for our new democracy.
One thing alone can disennoble us,
One thing destroy our vigour and our beauty,
One thing alone can have no place in Athens,
That one thing which I fear in you: despair.

SOPHOCLES You have prepared another city like us
Far on the western seas in Italy,
New Sybaris, where Hippodamos' pencil,
Trapped in the four corners of his mind,
Spreads his square net of streets; and Lampon peers;
Herodotos has joined them with the wealth
You gave him as his prize: a pan-Hellenic
Vision of Pericles—a second Athens?

PINDAR Radiant, crowned with violets, praised in song;
Noble, famed Athens, guardian of the Greeks,
Citadel of the gods: you must not fall!

KALLIAS One generation grows and falls like leaves,
And seed must die before the harvest sheaves.
Pericles, shall we face their threatening?

EURIPIDES Through all this glory I see suffering.

END OF ACT THREE

Act Four

SCENE ONE

EUANGELOS Euripides, are women allowed to join
In the cortège?

EURIPIDES No.

EUANGELOS Not even relatives—
Daughters, or widows? Mothers?

EURIPIDES Closely related
Women only are admitted to
The graveside, to lament.

EUANGELOS What was that tent
Taking up space in the Agora?

EURIPIDES The bones
Of those killed fighting for our city lie
In state for three days in the Agora,
Euangelos, in front of the monument
Of Eponyms. Each mourner comes to look,
And brings appropriate offering.

EUANGELOS How morbid!

EURIPIDES Why be repelled by others' sufferings?
Our city's greatness is it helps the helpless
For common justice; it accepts the law,
And honours gods of mercy. Here's true Athens:
Unnumbered men who fought, died, for our friends.

EUANGELOS The crowds are swelling. What's been happening?

EURIPIDES Ten coffins, each of cypress wood, were carried
On wagons in procession; one for each
Tribe of our city, filled with bones. And one
Empty, covered with a pall, for those
Whose bodies never will find burial.

EUANGELOS Where are they laid?

EURIPIDES In this most beautiful
Garden outside our city wall.

EUANGELOS They came
To this Kerameikos cemetery through
The Double Gates? Are all the war dead here?

EURIPIDES All? Not the men who died at Marathon.
Their supreme honour was to find last rest
On ground where they fell. A quiet mound's there now,
Peaceful and holy.

EUANGELOS Sophocles is armed!
Why are they here?

EURIPIDES The Athenian army, dressed
For battle leads the citizens and strangers
Down the broad road that slopes to our soft stream
That lulls the dead, Eridanos.

EUANGELOS I know!
We gather for the Panathenaic procession
Between the Sacred and the Double Gates,
Before we corner-cross the Agora
And climb up to Virgin Athene's home.

EURIPIDES Euangelos, today we walk the same
Path in the opposite direction.
These two processions weave the warp and weft
Of Athens' peplos.

EUANGELOS

Look! There's Pericles!
He walks out, slowly, from the tomb, and climbs
Up on the platform, high.

EURIPIDES

It has been built
So that his voice can reach as many people
As possible across this waiting crowd.
There's cockcrow on a distant hill. Now, listen.

SCENE TWO

PERICLES' *Oration.*

PERICLES

Most who have spoken in this place have praised
The man who added an oration to
Our ceremony; feel it right and good
A speech be made over the graves of those
Fallen for us in war. I should have liked
Such brave acts to have spoken for themselves:
Their courage would not then be at the mercy,
Blown power or feebleness of one man's words.
Some of you knew these fighters; how they died;
And loved them. You will find my words too pale.
To others here these men were scarcely known.
My praise will seem distorted, over-rich:
When someone's praised beyond what we could do,
Envy and unbelief sink piety.
But our ancestors thought this honour fit,
Appropriate; so I shall do my best
To speak no worse than you wish or expect.
Our forefathers deserve our praise. They gave us
A peaceful land down many generations;
And added to it, with their blood and courage,
An Empire handed now to us. We who
Are in the prime of life have held, expanded,
Strengthened and made to flower this
commonwealth
Until our city's self-sufficient for
Both peace and war. Before I praise the dead,
Let me remind you, citizens, allies, strangers,
That Athens' constitution is unique:

Worth dying for: created nowhere else,
Though imitated far. All power lies
With you, the many—not the easy few.
Each private case is equal in the law,
And public excellence in any field
Is crowned and honoured—not through privilege
But for innate ability. No one
Finds poverty a bar to public service.
In the same way, our private lives are free:
No one resents a neighbour's oddities,
But laughs, and welcomes rich diversity.
In private, tolerant; to laws respectful—
Especially those that protect the weak—
We give obedience to men we ask
To govern us. We honour unwritten laws
Which to neglect is disgrace. Look around!
Our relaxations beautify our souls
With sacrifices, festivals and games
Throughout the year. Even inside our homes
Our very pottery is elegant,
And gentle taste delights sadness away.
The goods of all the world flow into Athens—
Home-grown or foreign, you choose what you will:
And, in return, we do not send away,
Exile, expel or bar new foreigners,
Fear spies, or hoard state secrets; pry, and whisper.
The Spartans train from earliest childhood
To suffer pain. Perhaps it makes their lives
So miserable they throw them away
Gladly, in battle! But each of us lives
Happily; yet, when the testing comes,
Are we the less prepared to confront danger?
No! Look at our Empire! Yet, as well
As military might and unmatched courage,
We love all beauty with simplicity,
And wisdom, without weakness. Wealth is good,
An opportunity for action, use:
And poverty is no disgrace with us.
The only shame is laziness which fails
Even to attempt to rise above it. Here
The useless man who takes no interest
In politics has no true place at all:

For power rises from public discussion,
And words and deeds to us are not unlinked.
We ask for facts; debate; and then take action,
Rather than dash through ignorance to boldness.
It does no harm to estimate a risk.
True bravery is knowledge of the worst
Which, while it loves sweet life, still does not flinch;
Because the noble mind, when strong, gives favours,
And through goodwill earns friendship. Athens
alone
In time of trial outstrips expectation.
No enemy's ashamed to be defeated;
No subject can complain how he is ruled.
So Athens is the school of Hellas, graced.
We need no poet's fictions. Every sea
Is opened by our enterprise and daring;
And lands innumerable hold the graves,
Memorials of good done for our friends,
And our revenge on enemies. New years
To come, the future centuries will gaze
Astonished at us, as the present days
Admire and wonder.
Such, then, is the city
For which these men made their heroic choice
And died in battle. They could not bear the thought
She might be taken from them. Each of us,
Survivors, willingly should suffer for
Her sake. In praising Athens, I praise them.
It was their courage and their selflessness,
And of those like them, that made Athens great.
Some had their faults—but such an end dissolves
Away all private evils. One's own life
Given defending home and family
Reveals more goodness than our human failings.
They could have hung back, lived, grown rich. Not
one
Gave in to save his life. When hand-to-hand
Combat came, they fought through to the death.
True to our city these men died. We pray
That extreme test may not be ours: yet their
Spirit against the enemy must live.
We are their heirs. They died for us. You should

Fix your eyes every day on Athens' greatness
And become filled with love for her. When the vision
Inspires you, think: all this was won by these
Who gave the finest gift within their power:
Their breathing joy. Such praise shall not grow old.
The whole earth is a sepulchre of famous
Men. Their glory lives in memory
Unfading: for whenever elegy
Is celebrated, these shall be recalled
Beyond all epitaphs and monuments
To far, unwearied time. Emulate them;
For happiness depends on being free,
And freedom rests on courage. Cowardice
Is far more humbling than a sudden death.
A word of comfort, not commiseration,
To you, the parents of these men. In life
Those are the fortunate who gain most honour.
What greater honour is there than this end,
And for you to lament them? Happiness
And death are dealt and balanced—theirs,
complete.
I know it's difficult for you to feel this.
When you see others happy, you will be
Reminded. Yet, endure. Those who still can,
Breed further children to your comfort; they
Will fill both home and city. Only men
Whose children's lives are risked carry much weight
In fair and honest counsel. You, too old
Now to have children, may I ask you think:
The greater part of your days has been happy;
What's yet to come is brief. Only one thing,
The love of honour, is untouched by age,
And the last human pleasure is respect.
Sons and brothers of the fallen, you've
A hard life, now, for all men praise the dead.
Whatever you achieve will not come near
Their sacrifice. But try. And you, our widows;
Your glory is not to allow yourselves
To show more weakness than is natural
To your sex; and not be a cause for gossip,
Whether in praise or blame.

Under this winter
Sky I have obeyed our public custom.
One final tribute to those we now bury,
And then I end:
Until they come of age, their children will
Be maintained at the public cost: a garland
Substantial, with which Athens crowns her own.
Where virtue's most rewarded, there are found
The finest citizens. Now, when you've mourned
Your loved ones, each alone, you may depart.

SCENE THREE

As PERICLES *enters the crowd, the crowd place garlands round his neck, and shower him with flowers.*

ELPINIKE

Pericles, these flowers thrown to you
Plucked as they spread wide to the open day
Are the young lives of our brave, laughing men
Fresh in their bloom, cropped not in war against
The Medes and Persians, whom my Kimon fought,
But allies killing allies, Greek-hacked Greek.
Yes, this was a noble action, Pericles.
You deserve garlands.

PERICLES

Ah, Elpinike;
Anoint a younger head, not one that's grey.
Our city mourns a year that's lost its spring.

Exit PERICLES.

SOPHOCLES

There are some actions Pericles must take
To satisfy his party's outer wing,
And out-manoeuvre more extreme demands.
Megara's war he lifts out of their hands,
Endorsing it, to hold them from over-reaching
To Corfu, Sicily, a conquering route
Dreamed for new Empire in the Italian west.

ELPINIKE

Hermippos prosecutes Aspasia
For just this. You know what the gossip is:

Aspasia procured the black decree
Against the Megarid for personal spite.

SOPHOCLES Hermippos thinks his coarse, satiric plays,
And the attacks on Pericles' close friends,
Have loosened stones for undermining him
Through his Aspasia. She may not answer.
Pericles pleads on her behalf. He weeps.

ELPINIKE What are the formal charges?

SOPHOCLES She persuaded
Pericles help her native home, Miletus,
In fighting Samos, that island that expelled
Democracy. She often entertains
High, married ladies, wives of Athens' men,
Corrupting them; and educating to
An expectation for your sex which Athens
Has no room for, entirely out of place
And inappropriate . . .

ELPINIKE Our natural life
Needs men and woman, why not our public, too?

SOPHOCLES Seclusion is protection. Men must live
To die, if necessary, for the state.
Women must balance this, and live to breed
A family that serves the city's need.

SCENE FOUR

XANTHIPPOS Father, I have never seen you cry;
Certainly not in public.

PERICLES Xanthippos,
My son, I trust you never will again.
My enemies leave me but pluck my friends.
Damon exiled. Ephialtes killed.
Pheidias, mysteriously in prison
Found dead, though acquitted. Then my tutor,
Anaxagoras—taken by night by me

To a Lampsakos ship delivering wines
To Athens, going home, where loyal friends
Now care for his old age in their hill vineyard.
But this last trial, of Aspasia,
Once again, for 'impiety', showed all
They were not gardeners weeding irreligion
But a pack hunting vulnerability.
She could not answer: first, as alien
From far Miletus; secondly, as a woman.
They claimed she had persuaded me to help
Her home town; to have urged this new decree
That blocks the Megarid from Empire's markets
In punishment. What else did it expect?

XANTHIPPOS The Spartans use this new law as their quarrel
With Athens, say we cripple Megara.

PERICLES Megara was our friend: as such she slaughtered
Andokides' best men.

XANTHIPPOS Didn't Megarians
Steal two of Aspasia's prostitutes?
Isn't there some truth in the charge?

PERICLES My son,
Which is the greater—sun or moon? Just ask:
The lives and futures of our fighting troops,
The pride of Athens, or two hiring girls?
The other words they said disgraced the air
That carried them.

XANTHIPPOS Aspasia is acquitted.
I hear the jury were both shocked and moved.

PERICLES That shows the strength of our democracy.

XANTHIPPOS Those who seek power in our democracy
Are made unfit to hold it by the process.

PERICLES The rooted impulse to stability
Guides all life up to light!

XANTHIPPOS But by perverse
Self-will, we climb all hierarchy higher,
Rungs past our skills, till the gods kick us down.
How did you make the Spartans melt away?

PERICLES Bribed them: ten talents. Promised them
concessions,
And bought, not peace, but time.

XANTHIPPOS They will be back?

PERICLES Doubtless they will. Pleistoanax is fined
And sacked. Kleandridas his general fled,
Condemned to death in absence; his estates
Confiscated by Sparta.

XANTHIPPOS We'll use this lull?

PERICLES Their strength depends on land. We rule the seas.
Prepare the fleet, and make a sudden assault
Where it will hurt—at Epidauros. I
Will lead the triremes.

XANTHIPPOS Aegina has complained
To Sparta: Athens stops Megarian trade,
So interferes with her autonomy.

PERICLES That eyesore of Piraeus! One small island
Buzzing in our backyard for the enemy.
We'll make Aegina evacuation ground,
If farms and villages of Attica
Need to come in behind our Long Walls, safe
From the red cloaks and spears of Spartan crests.

XANTHIPPOS Father, you run the city wisely, well,
And have enhanced all lives, except our own.
The price of your success, integrity
With money, has been your own family.
You were away. Your estate's run by slaves;
And my wife, your own daughter-in-law, can't buy
The jewellery that other wives expect.
I've had to borrow money in your name;

And I can't possibly repay the debt.

PERICLES You and your wife contribute nothing—take
No interest in this city: mind your own
Business, till you've no busyness at all.
Athens in crisis is no place for gauderies.
Not only shall I not pay: I shall sue
The creditor who lent that sum to you.

XANTHIPPOS Father: when I was young I was ignored
By you. My elder brother had your thoughts.
My mother rightly went back to her man.
Look! Politics and war is not a world
For those who value their home life, their books.

PERICLES Peace must be earned, not borrowed. He who fails
Through lack of moral guts to care for gifts
Won by our parents' blood and pain, so we
Can hand an Empire to posterity,
Is just a fraudulent trustee for all
The freedom in good faith committed him.

XANTHIPPOS Father, I shall not speak to you again.

PERICLES Our daring, innovation, energy,
Our pride in all that Homer would have loved,
Our urge to fame and honour, you despise;
Yet cushion your weak spine with merchandise.

XANTHIPPOS Competitive, greedy, tyrannical
Aggression is how other states see us.
The Parthenon is hubris, misplaced skill:
And you won't even pay your own son's bill.

SCENE FIVE

PERICHORE I've looked so hard at this slow, shifting shadow
On the sundial. See the ants running in
And out like refugees on market day,
Scuttling for shade? But I can't see it move.

ASPASIA

Our patience is too limited, our lives
Too brief. Come, we must pack and bury jewels
Out in the garden—and remember where!
The Spartan army burns Acharnai village,
Led by old King Archidamos. The order
To evacuate all households is announced.
Athens pants with refugees. This heat
Breeds women-eating mosquitoes. Our wagon
Leaves now to reach the ship that's sailing south
Out to Aegina island. You must go—
Cattle and sheep are being ferried, too.

ETERAPOULA

Will there be shelter there for all of us?

ASPASIA

You two go on ahead, make some secure.
The people of Aegina have been moved
To Thyreatis, on to Spartan ground,
So all their farms and homes and emerald walks
Are ours for choosing.

PERICHORE

Oh what fun! I want
One by a stream that keeps my flax wet.

ETERAPOULA

I'll
Need a large oven in my house for pots.

ASPASIA

My baby needs less hustle round its cot,
Less tension in the air. I'll lose my milk
With worry if you don't give me rest soon.
There's a new temple on a shaded hill,
Built to their local goddess out of limestone
Set above woodland in a flower-pinned meadow.
Find us a cottage near, where I can look
Back past the gulf to Athens, see the smoke
Rise, as *he* did—a boy at Salamis:
Though may these fires burn with the Spartan dead.

ETERAPOULA

For us, power is flesh; for them it's killing.
How strange our role-playing is mocked and sneered,
While theirs is praised!

PERICHORE My flesh is irritating.
No, not like that! My eyes feel hot; my head's
On fire.

ASPASIA Your teeth are bleeding.

PERICHORE *coughs, badly.*

What a cough!

PERICHORE My stomach!

ETERAPOULA You've grown ulcers on your skin
Suddenly, like mushrooms.

PERICHORE Quick! I need water!
Anything! (*Exit*)

ETERAPOULA What strange gnat's been eating her?

ASPASIA You go, and sail her quickly to Aegina
Where she'll be safe. Here's no place to be ill.
The baby's woken! Shelter on that hill!

Exeunt.

SCENE SIX

KALLIAS King Archidamos—yes, your friend—has sent
Melesippos, his own ambassador,
Up to the walls to find you.

PERICLES Send him away.

KALLIAS We have; and said, if Sparta wants to talk,
Their army must disband, withdraw, and leave.

PERICLES Did Melesippos answer?

KALLIAS That this day
Brings a great cage of evils to all Greece.

SOPHOCLES It does. Plague rages through the refugees.

KALLIAS (*To* PERICLES) Perhaps go out and speak to them?

PERICLES Athenians!
Friends; and all who shelter in our care:
No city would bring war upon herself.
You know the facts; you thought, and voted for it,
As I did—though I know its horrors well:
But loss of freedom is a greater evil—
Slavery! Which we face. Never forget
Our navy's still the mightiest in the world.
Farmers, I know you've lost your crops, and land,
But time will give them back; and healing nature
Ripens forgetfulness as seasons pass.
We are not fighting for ourselves alone
But for an Empire, which our fathers gave us,
Who fought the might of Persia here, and won—
For you! Empire breeds hatred. It would be
Folly to slack our hold now. All who rule
Others will be unpopular at times;
And envy's the old payment. Hatred passes,
But glory outlives all, for ever haunts
The memories of men. We have the plague:
But so will they—and they are far from home.
They cannot breach our Long Walls; safe, and manned.
The seas are ours; and time is on our side.
One party talks appeasement, peace. Ignore them.
They sell our future for a day of ease,
The slave's mentality. Who stands at danger
Fully prepared to die as he protects
His children, wife, his gods, his land; his freedom?
I do. You do. We Athenians
Expect no less of each. There, Sparta's king
Is my old friend. They've burned your farms. If he
Has spared my country home for courtesy,
I give it to this city; yours, for ever,
Its parks and gardens . . .

DIOPEITHES Pericles! You have
Been stripped of Generalship today, and may
No longer speak.

PERICLES I am stripped of command?

DIOPEITHES Others take over now. And one thing more:
Your bookkeeping and finance are ignored.
Accountability in public men's
Essential. The date's past; and you are fined
Fifteen talents. Go! Your day is done.

SOPHOCLES Pericles; come with me. Athens will need you.
She's done the same to all her greatest men.
But I have sudden news. Your sons are dead;
Paralos and Xanthippos. Yes; the plague.
Also your sister, the priestess.

PERICLES Bear with me,
Sophocles. My sons? Both of the boys?
And my one sister, too? This carrion plague?
I've praised Athenian courage: now I need
A little strength myself. Thank you. The stones
(*Looking at the Parthenon*) Outlast our sadness,
but they do not feel it.
Please will you stay with me a moment, till
My eyes have cleared?

SOPHOCLES Pericles, of course.

SCENE SEVEN

KALLIAS Euangelos? Where have you come from, boy?
If from your master, you've arrived too soon.
Sophocles is addressing the Assembly,
Many of whom want Pericles re-elected
General; the war back in his hands.
Who else is there who knows the Spartan king,
And can be trusted to put Athens first
Rather than private profit? Who else has
His wisdom, vision and experience?

EUANGELOS Great Kallias; the plague! the plague!

KALLIAS Why, boy;
Who has it?

EUANGELOS I don't think my master does:
He's strong, though feverish: but plants are blighted,
And children poisoned from the reservoirs.
Even the household dogs run wild, and foam,
Lie on their backs, and howl. The stuffy huts
Of refugees along the walls are piled
With bodies, dead and dying. What god cares?
Those who were nursing spread disease, infected;
And no one has a funeral any more.
Each tips new bodies on the nearest pyre,
And lives in sudden wealth and sexual greed.
Law has collapsed, and outside Athens all
Is scorched earth.

KALLIAS Well, Archidamos knows plague
Could eat his army. He's gone on to Laurium,
Down on the cape.

SCENE EIGHT

EUANGELOS Aspasia is here.

Enter ASPASIA.

(*To* ASPASIA) The Spartans have retreated!

KALLIAS Not retreated;
Moved on for safety. (*Pause*)

ASPASIA Yes; he has the plague.

KALLAIS (*To* EUANGELOS) Run, and tell Sophocles, even if he's speaking.

Exit EUANGELOS.

Has Pericles lost his serenity?
Surely not!

ASPASIA You know him: in pain, but quiet
With a translucent clarity of mind.
Please will you see him? He's outside.

KALLIAS Of course.
I am an old man and prepared for death.
Plague or the sword make little difference now;
But Athens needs him desperately.

SCENE NINE

ASPASIA *brings in* PERICLES. *He wears a simple loincloth.*

ASPASIA Please; no clothes
Touching his shoulders. Sometimes he shakes.

PERICLES Kallias,
Perhaps we shall defeat the plague, and Spartans!
The will is there!

KALLIAS I know it is.

PERICLES Aspasia,
Your gentleness has made me great.

(ASPASIA *moves to embrace him, but is warned back from touching him by* PERICLES)

Protect
Yourself, and our young Pericles, from me.
May he survive and, ruling over men,
Be just and humble in the sight of God.
Then he shall be as morning light. His day
Cloudless. His subjects tender grass that springs
Up shining after rain. (*Pause*) His future is
My candle, as these eyes darken.

Enter SOPHOCLES.

KALLIAS Sophocles!

PERICLES They've tried to hang a charm on me. I must
Be ill to let them!

SOPHOCLES Well, the tide-blown vote's

Quicksilver. You're elected Commander-in-Chief
Again: in sole charge while the city stumbles.
The Spartans have struck camp, in fear of plague.
To help your grief, it seemed good to the Council
And People to make an exception for
Your natural son. He's made full citizen.

ASPASIA No child is illegitimate to its mother;
But this, my greatest hope's shot through like silk
With sickening fear . . . (*Gestures to* PERICLES)

SOPHOCLES Not the plague?

PERICLES Yes, it is.
Tell them Athens will be victorious
If she takes no risks—think of Kleinias:
If, while this war continues, she holds back
From further widening of Empire: if
She nurtures, above all, our ships and sailors;
And is not over-confident. Then she,
Holding to what she has, and growing stronger,
May face the worst with courage, and be free.

Enter EUANGELOS *with a letter.*

KALLIAS Here is a letter sent from Socrates
Who's heard, as all have, of your private griefs,
And of the mob's ingratitude.

PERICLES (*Tries to read it; fails*) Read for me.

KALLIAS (*Reads*) 'A just man in this life, were one to come,
Would be scourged, tortured, and imprisoned; his eyes
Burned out, and, after more humiliation,
He would no doubt be crucified. We both
Remember those words Aeschylus told Athens:
"To be just, not merely seem pure to crowds . . ."
Who has embodied that ideal, but you?'

PERICLES I always thought I should meet death in battle:
It seems lieutenant Socrates has fresh
Ideas for me! But he's too generous.
The plague's just as effective. Aspasia,
You must marry, a young, stronger husband

Who can protect you now that I am gone;
And may you both, and my small future fragment,
On the far shore beyond catastrophe,
Have sunny days of unimpeded calm.

PERICLES *drops his head.*

ASPASIA He's not retreated from his brightness.

KALLIAS No.
When we remember that as General
He's won nine major victories for Athens . . .

PERICLES Don't celebrate my battlefields. Just say
No Athens mother ever mourned a son
Because of negligence by me.

KALLIAS That's true.
He held his men's lives, never squandered them.
His spirit flickers.

ASPASIA Pericles!

KALLIAS He goes.

PERICLES *dies.*

SOPHOCLES Light and shadow are intermingled, dappled.
It was no bolt from Zeus that took him. Just
A gentle, painless breath: a butterfly
Of trembling lips—then peace.

EUANGELOS (*Suddenly aware*) He's dead!

ASPASIA He is.
A golden afternoon has shed its wonder
Across our years. No one can ask for more.

KALLIAS Please leave his body. No one else but he
Of all men in our time that I have known
Had the true wisdom of simplicity:
Honest, and selfless—only he, alone.

END OF ACT FOUR

EPILOGUE

SOPHOCLES *comes forward.*

Here, beyond all stormy seas,
Lies Olympian Pericles.
As he was my perfect friend
Shed no tears now at his end.
All he ever hoped from Fate
Was that Athens might create
An example to all Greece
In a world that honours peace,
Where democracy's elect
Show each citizen respect
Till the city harmonize
Eternal temples to the skies.
Men and women will shed tears
Over him two thousand years
And go on, inspired to learn
Something at his ruined urn.
Now his vision's been retold;
See him overwhelmed and cold.
Till a mortal life's complete,
Past all triumph and defeat,
Wait, before you call him blest,
Till he's found his final rest.

FINIS

Contemporary Classic

Philippa Logan's review of Healing Nature.

(Oxford Mail, 21.xi.87)

A real treat in poetry was to be had in the Sheldonian last night. This was the première performance of *Healing Nature*, by Francis Warner, Vice-Master of St. Peter's College, Oxford. Subtitled *The Athens of Pericles*, the play is about the turmoil that the birth pangs of democracy bring to a city, and the revolution and hostilities that accompany it.

Francis Warner's play was safe in the hands of the Oxford University Dramatic Society, who, under the direction of Mark Payton, put on a classically Greek production. Mark Payton himself played a sympathetic Sophocles, full of warmth and advice for his friend Pericles, who was admirably portrayed by Rob Smith.

Good acting too came from Bethany Bell as Perichore, the prostitute; and all brought out the Shakespearian quality of the play's verse and depth of meaning.

Mr Warner must have been well pleased with the performance and its reception. And there could have been no better setting than the magnificent amphitheatre that is the Sheldonian.

Athens of a Master Dramatist

Review by Geordie Greig of The Sunday Times in

THE STAGE, 17.iii.88

In *Healing Nature: The Athens of Pericles*, presented at its gala première in the Sheldonian Theatre by the Oxford University Dramatic Society, Francis Warner, the Oxford poet and dramatist, has given vivid expression to the triumphs and tragedies during the rise and fall of Athens' great empire during the fifth century B.C.

The action centres round Pericles, the aristocratic general, commandingly played by Rob Smith, as he creates 'an Athens all the world will imitate', only to see the tide of fortune turn and the empire fall into decay. It is a compelling play which combines the grand, heroic drama of Marlowe's *Tamburlaine* with moments of exquisitely delicate lyric poetry and unexpected dashes of humour.

Mr Warner has shown once more he is a masterful poet and dramatist. *Healing Nature*, his eleventh play, is his best work to date. Its exploration of the dilemmas facing empire-builders and empire-losers is original, thought-provoking, and relevant.

The director Mark Payton purposely uses simplicity and formality to full effect in his production in the Sheldonian Theatre; the first play to be performed there for nearly three hundred years.

The production was also enhanced by David Colmer's skilful lighting, which at times gave an almost Rembrandt-like quality and atmosphere to the tragedy being played in Sir Christopher Wren's building.

Payton also played Sophocles, the Athenian dramatist and general, and demonstrated a huge wealth of talent. Francis Warner's play and its cast of nineteen deserve high praise.